· The What's Inside Library™ ·

What's Inside the Moon?

Jane Kelly Kosek

The Rosen Publishing Group's
PowerKids Press™
New York

For Kelly—know that small steps toward greatness can lead to giant achievements.
Special thanks to Christopher H. Starr at the Pacific-Sierra Research Corporation.

Published in 1999 by The Rosen Publishing Group, Inc.
29 East 21st Street, New York, NY 10010

First Edition

Book Design: Kim Sonsky

Photo Credits: Cover, back cover, title page, pp. 5, 14, 17, 18 © Digital Vision Ltd.; contents page and p. 6 © FPG International/Christian Michaels; p. 10 © FPG International/Telegraph Colour Library; p. 11 © FPG International/NASA 1984; p. 18 International Stock/K. H. Photo; p. 22 © FPG International/NASA 1991.

Kosek, Jane Kelly.
    What's inside the moon?/ Jane Kelly Kosek.
        p.   cm. — (What's inside library)
    Includes index.
    Summary: Discusses the layers, rocks, phases and other aspects of the moon and examines
    our exploration of it.
    ISBN 0-8239-5282-7
    1. Moon—Internal structure—Juvenile literature. 2. Moon—Juvenile literature.
    [1. Moon.] I. Title. II. Series: Kosek, Jane Kelly. What's inside library.
    QB592.K67 1998
    559.9'1—dc21   98-11742
                                                                          CIP
                                                                          AC

Manufactured in the United States of America

Contents

Where Did the Moon Come From?

The Moon is the brightest object in our night sky. It is about 238,000 miles from our planet Earth. Scientists are not exactly sure where the Moon came from. But they do have some ideas. Most scientists think the Moon is the result of a **collision** (kuh-LIH-zhun) between Earth and a smaller planet. This collision probably happened about 4.5 billion years ago. Scientists believe that the collision caused objects to shoot out into space. The Moon may have been formed from these objects.

The Moon is about four times smaller than Earth. Since the Moon was formed, it has been **orbiting** (OR-bih-ting), or circling, Earth. It takes 27 days, 7 hours, and 43 minutes for the Moon to travel all the way around Earth.

Other planets have many moons orbiting around them, but Earth only has one. ▷

What Is the Moon Made Of?

Some people have said that the Moon is made of Swiss cheese. This is because there are lots of holes on the Moon's **surface** (SER-fiss). These holes are called **craters** (KRAY-terz).

The Moon may look like a big piece of cheese, but it is actually made of many different kinds of rocks. Most of the rocks were formed from the collision between Earth and a smaller planet. Other rocks were formed from very large objects that hit the Moon more than 3 billion years ago and left their mark on its surface.

◁ Long ago, people thought that the moon was made of cheese because they had no way of studying it. Today we know better.

The Moon's Layers

The Moon's layers consist of a **mantle** (MAN-tul) and **crust** (KRUST). Scientists are not sure, but they believe the Moon also may have a **core** (KOR). The core is the center of the Moon. The mantle surrounds the core, and the crust rests on top of the mantle.

There is no **atmosphere** (AT-mus-feer), or layer of gases, on the Moon. Without an atmosphere, the Moon's **temperature** (TEMP-rah-chur) changes from less than −200° F to more than 200° F. Humans need to wear space suits when they're on the Moon in order to breathe. The Moon has a black sky—not blue, like on Earth. Also, there is no weather, such as rain or snow, on the Moon.

So far, water has not been found on the Moon's surface. ▷
But scientists continue to search for the truth.

The Core

We are able to study the Moon up close because **astronauts** (AS-truh-nots) have visited it. From their studies, scientists have decided that the Moon most likely has a core made of iron. This is kind of like Earth's core, which is made of iron and nickel. But the Moon's core is much smaller than Earth's core. The Moon's core is about 800 miles below the surface of the Moon. And its core is a little bit off center. It is thought to be only about 500 miles across. Scientists believe that a layer of partly-liquid rock surrounds the Moon's core.

◁ When American astronauts first visited the Moon in 1969, they planted an American flag.

11

The Mantle

The mantle is the layer between the core and crust. It is about 40 to 60 miles below the surface of the Moon. The mantle is the Moon's largest layer. It is about 750 miles thick and is made of rock. More than 3 billion years ago, hot liquid rock, called **magma** (MAG-muh), was released from the mantle through cracks in the crust. It flowed into large craters that had formed when large space objects hit the Moon's surface. The magma in these craters formed seas of **lava** (LAH-vuh). The lava has since cooled into solid rocks called **basalts** (buh-SALTS). A 17th-century **astronomer** (uh-STRON-uh-mer) named Galileo thought these basalt-filled craters looked like seas of water, so he called them *maria*, which means "seas" in the Latin language.

Scientists used to think the Moon was the same inside as on its surface. Now they know that the moon has different layers. ▷

CRUST

CORE

PARTLY
MELTED
ROCK

MANTLE

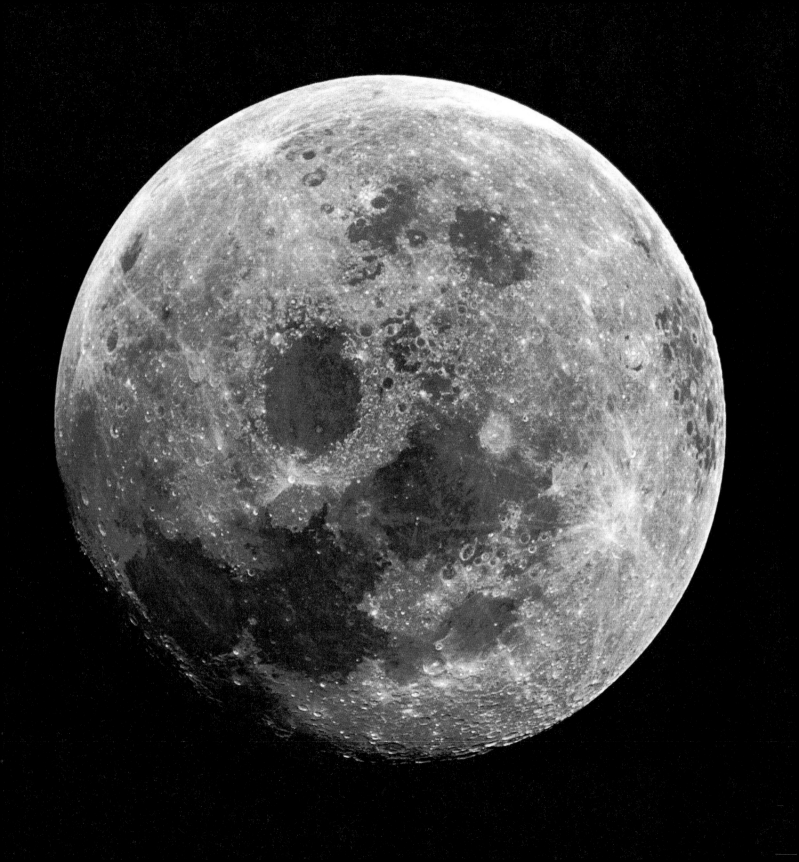

The Crust

The Moon's crust is thicker on one side than on the other. But we only see one side of the Moon. This is because the Moon spins once on its **axis** (AK-sis) at the same speed as it travels around Earth. The crust on the side that faces Earth is about 40 miles thick. The crust on the other side of the Moon is about 60 miles thick. A layer of powder-like soil called **regolith** (REH-guh-lith) covers the crust.

There are also light and dark areas on the Moon. The light areas make up most of the Moon's surface. They are called **terrae** (teh-RAY), or highlands. The dark areas are the *maria*, or lowlands. The highlands have many craters and are the oldest parts of the Moon. The *maria* are the large basalt-filled craters. They are found mainly on the side of the Moon that faces Earth.

◁ When we look at the moon and see dark, empty areas, we are really seeing the *maria*.

15

The Moon's Craters

The Moon's craters were made when large space objects slammed into the Moon. Most of the major collisions occurred during the Moon's first billion years. In the last 3 billion years, the Moon hasn't changed much.

The Moon's craters are all different sizes. Some are so small that you cannot see them. Very large craters are called **impact basins** (IM-pakt BAY-sinz). The largest crater on the Moon is called South Pole Aitken. It is found on the far side of the Moon and is 1,550 miles across. The far side of the Moon has the most craters.

Some craters are so large they can be seen from Earth. Others are so small they can only be seen with a telescope. ▷

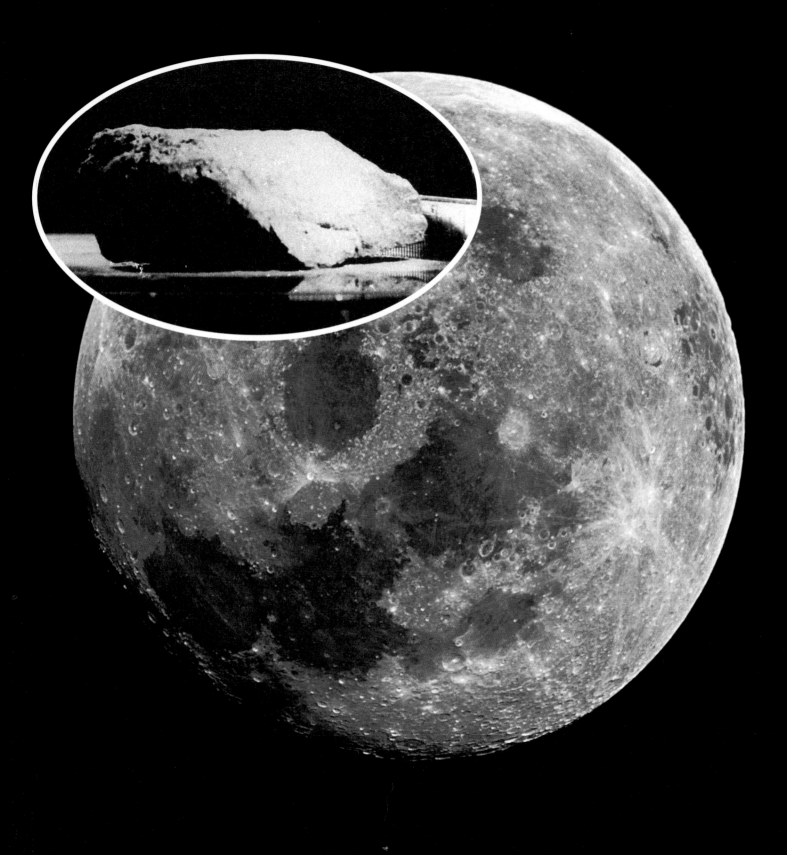

Moon Rocks

Astronauts first visited the Moon in 1969. They brought back many different kinds of Moon rocks for scientists to study. The rocks were taken from different areas on the Moon, including the regolith, *maria*, and terrae. These rocks have told us a lot about the Moon.

Moon rocks do not have any water in them. This tells us that as far as we know, the Moon has never had any water on it. All the rocks studied are between 3 and 4.5 billion years old. Because they are so old, we can also learn something about the history of the **solar system** (SOH-ler SIS-tem) from these rocks.

◁ Moon rocks, such as the one on the left, were taken from the surface of the Moon to be studied on Earth.

Moonlight

   Did you know that moonlight does not come from inside the Moon? It is actually light from the sun reflected from the Moon's surface. The sun lights up half the Moon all the time. The part of the Moon that we see lit up depends on where the Moon is in its orbit around Earth. On some nights the Moon is not **visible** (VIH-zih-buhl). This is because the sun is lighting up the side of the Moon that we cannot see from Earth. This is called the new Moon. As the Moon continues to orbit Earth, more of the Moon can be seen. Halfway through the Moon's orbit, we can see the whole side of the Moon facing Earth. This is called the full Moon. As the Moon continues through its orbit, less of the Moon can be seen. It becomes a new Moon again and repeats the **cycle** (SY-kul).

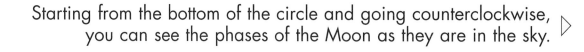

Starting from the bottom of the circle and going counterclockwise, you can see the phases of the Moon as they are in the sky.

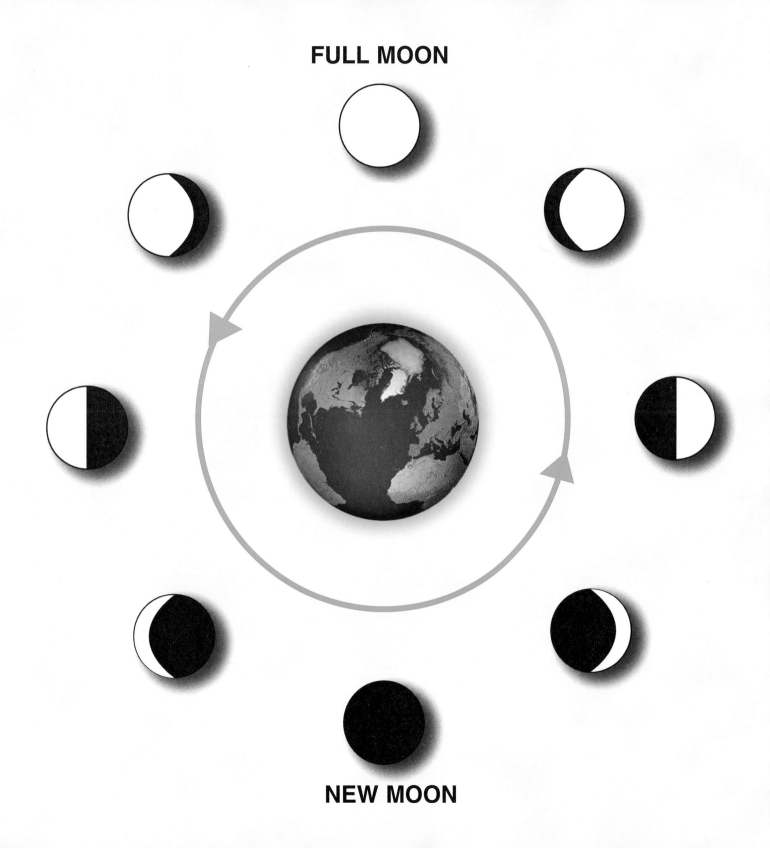

FULL MOON

NEW MOON

Humans on the Moon

The Moon is the only other space object, besides Earth, on which humans have walked. There is less **gravity** (GRAV-ih-tee) on the Moon than on Earth. This means that if you weigh about 60 pounds on Earth, you would only weigh about 10 pounds on the Moon. In July 1969 astronauts were sent for the first time in a spacecraft to the Moon. Neil Armstrong and Edwin "Buzz" Aldrin were the first two astronauts to step onto the Moon's surface. This was an incredible **achievement** (uh-CHEEV-ment) for humankind. From this **mission** (MI-shun) and others, scientists continue to learn more about the Moon and what's inside it.

Web Sites:

To find out more about the Moon, check out these Web sites:
http://ess.geology.ufl.edu/ess/Notes/020-Intro_ESS/Assign1/luna.html
http://web.eecs.nwu.edu/~pred/TNP/nineplanets/luna.html

Glossary

achievement (uh-CHEEV-ment) Something that is often done with courage and is recognized.

astronaut (AS-truh-not) A person who travels in space.

astronomer (uh-STRON-uh-mer) A person who studies space.

atmosphere (AT-mus-feer) A layer of gases around an object in space.

axis (AK-sis) An imaginary line that runs through the Moon and on which it turns.

basalt (buh-SALT) A rock on the Moon's surface formed from lava.

collision (kuh-LIH-zhun) When two or more things hit one another very hard.

core (KOR) The center of the Moon.

crater (KRAY-ter) Holes on the surface of the Moon.

crust (KRUST) The outer layer of the Moon.

cycle (SY-kul) A series of events that are repeated in the same order.

gravity (GRAV-ih-tee) A force between two objects that causes them to be attracted to each other.

impact basin (IM-pakt BAY-sin) A very large crater on the Moon's surface.

lava (LAH-vuh) What magma is called when it reaches the Moon's surface.

magma (MAG-muh) Hot, liquid rock inside the Moon's mantle.

mantle (MAN-tul) The layer of the Moon that is between the core and the crust.

mission (MI-shun) Being sent on a special trip.

orbiting (OR-bih-ting) When one thing is circling another.

regolith (REH-guh-lith) The layer of soil covering the Moon's crust.

solar system (SOH-ler SIS-tem) The system made up of our sun, the nine planets, moons, and other space objects.

surface (SER-fiss) The top or outside of something.

temperature (TEMP-rah-chur) How hot or cold something is.

terrae (teh-RAY) The highlands, which are the oldest areas on the Moon's surface.

visible (VIH-zih-buhl) Able to be seen.

Index